YOUR KNOWLEDGE HAS VALUE

Bibliographic information published by the German National Library:

The German National Library lists this publication in the National Bibliography; detailed bibliographic data are available on the Internet at http://dnb.dnb.de .

Imprint:

Copyright © 2015 GRIN Verlag, Open Publishing GmbH
Print and binding: Books on Demand GmbH, Norderstedt Germany
ISBN: 9783668418479

This book at GRIN:

http://www.grin.com/en/e-book/355382/humanitarian-logistics-which-challenges-do-aid-agencies-have-to-face-in

Stefan Lehrer

Humanitarian Logistics. Which challenges do aid-agencies have to face in disaster relief operations and how can these operations be efficient?

Based on South-East Asia 2004

GRIN Publishing

GRIN - Your knowledge has value

Since its foundation in 1998, GRIN has specialized in publishing academic texts by students, college teachers and other academics as e-book and printed book. The website www.grin.com is an ideal platform for presenting term papers, final papers, scientific essays, dissertations and specialist books.

Visit us on the internet:

http://www.grin.com/

http://www.facebook.com/grincom

http://www.twitter.com/grin_com

BACHELOR PAPER

Humanitarian Logistics

Which challenges do aid-agencies have to face in disaster relief operations and how can these operations be efficient? Based on South-East Asia 2004

submitted at:

FH JOANNEUM Gesellschaft mbH

Fachhochschulstudiengang

Management internationaler Geschäftsprozesse

(Bachelor)

submitted by:

Stefan Lehrer

Abstract

This paper investigates the theory of humanitarian logistics and in further consequence the disaster relief operation during the tsunami catastrophe in South-East Asia 2004.

The objective of the paper is to define the differences between commercial logistics and humanitarian logistics and to analyze the efficiency of the disaster relief operation in South-East Asia 2004.

The first part of this paper focuses on theoretical implications and deals, among others, with the definition of humanitarian logistics. Further, the differences of humanitarian logistics and commercial logistics will be analyzed based on the previous discussed definition. Moreover, the different objectives of humanitarian logistics and commercial logistics as well as the challenges of cooperation and coordination based on the high number of actors involved need to be emphasized.

Part 2 of this paper analyzes the disaster relief operation in the crisis region of South-East Asia. In order to do so, the disaster relief response and its potential for improvement will be segmented and analyzed in three phases consisting of preparation, immediate response and reconstruction. Insufficiencies of every phase will be explained. While researching for this paper it became obvious that the risk of a tsunami was neglected in terms of preparation. During the phase of immediate response, deficiencies concerning cooperation and coordination led to insufficiencies in the disaster relief operation. The phase of reconstruction focuses on tsunami-specific challenges. The main developments in the South-East Asian region since the tsunami-catastrophe in 2004 will be mentioned.

The **key words** of this paper are: humanitarian logistics, commercial logistics, disaster management, South-East Asia 2004, preparation for the tsunami in 2004, coordination in disaster relief operations and resource availability during tsunami 2004.

Kurzfassung

Die vorliegende Bakkalaureatsarbeit befasst sich mit humanitärer Logistik in der Theorie und in weiterer Folge mit dem humanitären Hilfseinsatz, welcher im Zuge der Tsunamikatastrophe in Südostasien stattgefunden hat.

Die Zielsetzung der Arbeit ist es, die Unterschiede zwischen kommerzieller und humanitärer Logistik zu definieren und den humanitären Hilfseinsatz in Südostasien bezüglich Effektivität zu analysieren.

Teil 1 der Bakkalaureatsarbeit besteht aus relevanter Theorie und befasst sich unter anderem mit der Definition von humanitärer Logistik. Darauf aufbauend werden die Unterschiede von Humanitärer Logistik und kommerzieller Logistik analysiert. Besonders hervorzuheben hierbei sind die unterschiedliche Zielsetzung sowie die Schwierigkeiten der Kooperation und Koordination aufgrund der Vielzahl an Beteiligten bei humanitären Einsätzen.

Der 2. Teil der Bakkalaureatsarbeit befasst sich mit einer Analyse des humanitären Einsatzes im Krisengebiet Südostasien. Hierbei werden der Hilfseinsatz und dessen Verbesserungspotenzial in drei Phasen, bestehend aus Vorbereitung, Sofortreaktion und Wiederaufbau, durchleuchtet. Unzulänglichkeiten in jeder Phase werden hervorgehoben und begründet. In der Phase der Vorbereitung ist offensichtlich, dass die Risiken einer Tsunamikatastrophe unterschätzt wurden. Während der Sofortreaktion sorgten Mängel in der Kooperation und Koordination dafür, dass die Effizienz des Hilfseinsatzes mangelhaft war. Für die Phase des Wiederaufbaus werden verschiedene, Tsunami-spezifische Schwierigkeiten analysiert. Abschließend wird die Weiterentwicklung seit der Tsunamikatastrophe 2004 thematisiert.

Schlüsselwörter dieser Arbeit sind: humanitäre Logistik, kommerzielle Logistik, Katastrophen Management, Südostasien 2004, Vorbereitung für Tsunami 2004, Koordination bei Katastropheneinsätzen und Ressourcenverfügbarkeit während Tsunami 2004.

Table of Contents

1. Introduction

If earthquakes, floods, avalanches, tsunamis or civil wars, catastrophes often have radical consequences for people living in the affected areas. Due to the constant increase of natural and manmade disasters, attention for disaster relief operations has become noticeable.

In the past 30 years the average number of natural disasters has risen from 125 up to approximately 500 per annum. Experts' state that the number of natural and human-made disasters will increase fivefold within the next 50 years; hence the need for efficient disaster relief operations is inevitable. (Maon, Lindgreen, & Vanhamme, 2009)

Rapid urbanization and environmental degradation are two of the main causes for the fact that the Asian region accounts for 89 percent of people affected by natural catastrophes. Between 1993 and 2003 disasters had a direct impact for approximately two billion people worldwide. (Perry, 2007)

The large number of people affected shows the importance of humanitarian aid agencies. In the case of a catastrophe the speed of humanitarian aid depends on the logistician's ability to establish a supply chain and deliver essential goods to troubled regions in the shortest time possible. (Kovács & Spens, 2007)

Effectiveness and efficiency in supplying medicines and goods necessary for survival is essential in the event of a disaster. Several statistics prove the central position of logistics in disaster operations by stating that logistics efforts account for 80 percent of disaster relief costs. (Abidi, de Leeuw, & Klumpp, 2014)

Although logistics is a significant expense factor in disaster relief operations, its importance was undervalued for many years. Since the tsunami hit South-East Asia in 2004 the attention for adequate logistics in humanitarian aid operations has increased. (Kovács & Spens, 2007)

2. Humanitarian Logistics

The term "humanitarian logistics" allows a broad interpretation; therefore experts determined several different definitions. An applicable approach is to consider humanitarian logistics as a process to mobilise people, resources, skills and knowledge with the aim to help those affected by a disaster. (Whiting & Ayala-Öström, 2009)

A more detailed description was made by Thomas and Mizushima (2005) by stating that humanitarian logistics is "the process of planning, implementing and controlling the efficient, cost-effective flow and storage of goods and materials, as well as related information, from point of origin to point of consumption for the purpose of meeting the end beneficiary´s requirements".

According to Chandes and Paché (2010) humanitarian logistics combines service and manufacturing. On one site the support of aid workers with the aim to optimize the delivery process for lifesaving goods can be assigned to service. On the other side the optimization of the delivery process requires a great deal of capabilities such as material and technological resources for transport- or warehousing activities. Therefore, humanitarian logistics also includes a manufacturing component.

By comparing humanitarian logistics with business logistics similarities in the basic principles are identifiable. Managing the flow of goods, information and finances from a specific source to the final customer is applicable for both types. In addition, various activities included in commercial logistics such as planning and procurement or transporting and warehousing remain in its ultimate elements also valid for humanitarian logistics. (Kovács & Spens, 2007)

To recap the statement above, one can determine that some similarities between both kinds of logistics exist. Nevertheless, by considering the basic principles more detailed, the list of differences is more comprehensive and will be discussed in the following.

3. Differences between Humanitarian Logistics and Commercial Logistics

When dealing with a catastrophe, logisticians in the humanitarian field need to be aware of several different challenges that basically do not exist in a commercial context.

Most of the time, crises have negative impacts on the infrastructure of the affected region. Based on the infrastructural issues, chaotic circumstances arise. Furthermore, high cooperative efforts as well as sudden and instable demands keep logisticians busy.

Due to these and many other characteristics, the main purpose of humanitarian logistics differs from its commercial counterpart.

3.1. Determining the Purpose of Humanitarian Logistics and Commercial Logistics

Defining the main purpose of both kinds of logistics leads to an understanding for the difference between humanitarian logistics and commercial logistics.

Deciding therefore is the importance of profitability. Langley and Rutner (2000) mentioned in their work about commercial logistics that the value of logistics lies in "the contribution to profitability". Therefore, the focus concerning business logistics is on cost reduction while the main purpose for logisticians in the humanitarian context is to ensure aid for people located in crisis regions.

As an example: Reacting as quickly as possible to a disaster often requires the use of airplanes but aerial transportation causes high costs. Thus, cost reduction plays a subordinated role in the phase of immediate response. (Baumgartner & Blome, 2014)

The term "profit" in a humanitarian context is directly linked to agencies benefactor´s; inefficient use of resources may lead to losses of donations, hence the profit depends on a donor's satisfaction. To secure a high efficiency, an approach to standardize processes would be helpful. (Chandes & Paché, 2010)

3.2. The issue of standardizing processes

Standardized processes are one of the key elements for many companies to achieve success therefore the desire to standardize processes for humanitarian logistics is obvious.

The fact that the dimension and the geographical area differ from disaster to disaster makes standardizing procedures in humanitarian logistics complicated. Moreover, humanitarian agencies have to employ their disaster relief systems in chaotic, uncertain environments with short lead times. (Fawcett & Fawcett, 2013)

To establish action rules in terms of emergency response implicit and explicit knowledge should be collected from situations already experienced in crises regions. Due to a high turnover of logisticians in the humanitarian context, a loss of experience whenever a logistician leaves is unavoidable. In addition, it is difficult to translate experiences made in one geographical area for decision makers in another geographical area. (Chandes & Paché, 2010)

Furthermore, many experts share the opinion that the constantly changing operational environment of humanitarian aid makes a complete standardization of processes impossible. (Chandes & Paché, 2010)

3.3. Unpredictable demand

Unpredictability of demand is ascribed to the fact that a great number of disasters are unforeseeable. The uncertainty in estimating when, where and to what extent a disaster occurs is a challenging factor for logisticians in disaster relief operations. (Kovács & Spens, 2007)

In the aftermath of a catastrophe a sudden occurrence of demand in large amounts emerges. (Kovacs & Spens, 2009) An increase in demand in turn requires an exceptional use of resources, but resources are limited by nature, therefore shortages, especially in complex disaster projects, arise. (Chang, Wilkinson, Potangaroa, & Seville, 2012)

To avoid such shortages, resources must be utilised as efficient as possible. Nevertheless, an anticipation of the exact demand is impossible; hence reaching total efficiency is excludable. (Scholten, Sharkey, & Fynes, 2010)

In order to be able to reduce the importance of an exact demand-anticipation successfully, organisations started to preposition resources. More precise, these resources are traceable in regions more prone to be affected by a natural or manmade catastrophe. (Kovács & Spens, 2007)

3.4.   Infrastructure

In general, disaster relief operations of humanitarian agencies follow the same procedure: At the beginning the focus is on establishing and optimizing the delivery process for the first urgent emergency care. Subsequently, rebuilding the destroyed infrastructure to guarantee a sustainable supply becomes more important. (Chandes & Paché, 2010)

Within the disaster-affected region, aid agencies need to be prepared for the worst: Bridges and air fields are potentially destroyed and hinder an adequate supply. Furthermore, a possibly damaged electricity network would have a negative impact on the communication infrastructure. (Kovacs & Spens, 2009)

If the communication infrastructure does not allow a permanent transfer of information, route planning becomes very challenging for logisticians. (Kovacs & Spens, 2009) In extreme situations, supplying goods by land is not possible. As a last resort, humanitarian aid agencies can make use of aircrafts to airdrop supplies. (Kovács & Spens, 2007)

Another issue in terms of infrastructure is the problem of the last mile. For instance, due to a destabilized infrastructure including limited power supplies, an appropriate temperature control for medicines can sometimes not be ensured. (Kovács & Spens, 2007)

3.5. Performance Measurement

A general belief in terms of efficiency and effectiveness is that companies, which apply performance measurement, outperform those that do not. Thus, measuring performance is crucial for an efficient and effective management of the humanitarian supply chain. (Abidi, de Leeuw, & Klumpp, 2014)

The function of performance measurement lies in the quantification of the efficiency and effectiveness of an operation. Therefore, specific indicators, such as capacity utilization, get determined. (Abidi, de Leeuw, & Klumpp, 2014)

Although measuring the performance brings advantages such as a simplification of the communication between supply chain actors, many humanitarian aid agencies fail to implement convincing key figures. For instance, an important part of humanitarian aid is to reduce suffering, but quantifying a relation between supply chain performance and alleviation of suffering is highly complex. (Abidi, de Leeuw, & Klumpp, 2014)

In addition, logisticians have to deal with various critical elements that complicate the measurement of performance in humanitarian supply chains. Among others, humanitarian aid agencies operate in a chaotic environment with a limited information technology capacity and infrastructure. Therefore, reliable data collection is problematic. (Abidi, de Leeuw, & Klumpp, 2014)

Evidence, that a general lack of motivation to measure performance in the non-profit sector exists, is shown in research: Only 20 per cent of the humanitarian organisations measure performance consistently while 55 per cent do not monitor and report performance measurement indicators at all. The remaining 25 per cent of the humanitarian aid agencies only use a few indicators. (Abidi, de Leeuw, & Klumpp, 2014)

Regarding performance measurement, development potential is given. Humanitarian organisations need to increase their research efforts in this respect to ensure continuous performance-improvement in disaster relief operations.

4. Actors

One special characteristic of humanitarian logistics is the broad range of actors participating in disaster relief operations. Principally, actors involved are: governments, international and national donors, international and regional organisations, international and national non-governmental organisations, police and armed forces, logistics service providers and the local population. (Sheppard, Tatham, Fisher, & Gapp, 2013)

In general, these different actors have the common goal to alleviate the suffering of vulnerable people. However, every actor has its own approach on how to reach this aim. Different approaches on how to reach a common goal, in turn, hamper humanitarian aid immense. (Kovács & Spens, 2007)

4.1.   Cooperation

A major problem that hinders the achievement of a better cooperation between humanitarian aid agencies is the constant expansion within the humanitarian sector. The high number of humanitarian organisations either leads to a competition environment for scarce donor resources rather than it leads to a performance improvement. (Abidi, de Leeuw, & Klumpp, 2014)

As a solution for this dilemma, experts suggest a more collaborative approach in terms of emergency response. Concerning shared equipment, assets or resources, collaboration among agencies improved in recent years, nevertheless, a lack of communication is still remaining. Often communication based problems arise before a disaster occurs since humanitarian organisations usually do not share information about available capabilities. (Maon, Lindgreen, & Vanhamme, 2009)

Fawcett and Fawcett (2013) assign the unwillingness of aid agencies to share information to the human nature by stating that "people perceive information as a source of power and legitimacy. As a result, they may be unwilling to share information that empowers others to their own potential detriment." With other words, the quest for limited resources in combination with the possibility to establish relationships to acquire them, leads to counterproductive information-sharing behaviour.

4.2. Coordination

Beside an existing lack of cooperation, insufficient coordination due to the high number of actors is trigging the overall success of a disaster relief operation. Estimations state, that 30.000 non-governmental organisations exist. (Tatham & Pettit, 2010) The fact that these organisations tend to manage their own created supply chains, which they developed over many years, makes a coordination of materials and human resources between organisations highly challenging. (Chandes & Paché, 2010)

The problem-solving approach regarding coordination lays in the development and expansion of collaborative information technology tools. However, a lack of considering the importance for supply chain management in disaster relief operations combined with the action-focused cultures of aid agencies hinder the development of information systems, information technology and logistics systems. (Maon, Lindgreen, & Vanhamme, 2009)

4.2.1. Limitation of Information Technology

Synchronisation of processes is very difficult due to discrepancies about appropriate processes among humanitarian agencies. As a result, regular planning in disaster relief supply chains is frequently lacking. For instance, central data bases that include information about transit times, prices paid or quantities purchased and received, do often not exist. (Maon, Lindgreen, & Vanhamme, 2009)

In recent years constitutions, such as the United Nations Joint Logistics Centre, have realised the importance of information technology in emergency aid by providing a common information platform. This platform supports organisations in terms of gathering, collating, analysing and disseminating logistics information in the phase before a disaster occurs. (Whiting & Ayala-Öström, 2009)

There is another indicator for a positive development concerning information technology systems in the humanitarian sector. Aid agencies started to create specialized common systems that contain information such as tracking and tracing. These systems are opened up for the use by other organisations. (Kovács & Spens, 2011)

5. Application of the Theoretical Knowledge to South-East Asia 2004

In the morning of December 26 in 2004, an earthquake, whose epicentre was located 160 kilometres off the northwest coast of Sumatra (Fagotto, 2014), had been measured with a Richter scale magnitude up to 9.3. The earthquake, known as Sumatran-Andaman quake, led to a movement of some places up to 15 meters. (Phillips, Nael, Wikle, Subanthore, & Hyrapiet, 2008)

This earthquake triggered a series of waves with a height up to 30 meters and thus caused the Indian Ocean Tsunami, which destroyed the coasts of 15 countries along the Indian Ocean. As a result, estimations state that more than 280.000 people were killed and 1.600.000 people became homeless. (Fagotto, 2014)

An event of this dimension brings along devastating short term impacts, extensive recovery and rebuilding efforts and long-lasting physical and societal re-organization. In addition, communities have to cope with socio economical problems such as a lack of productivity due to fatalities or poverty among widows and children. (Wiek, Ries, Thabrew, Brundiers, & Wickramasinghe, 2010)

The size of the Indian Ocean Tsunami in combination with its consequences led to the largest response in the history of humanitarian aid. (Neri, Scuteri, & Miniati, 2008)

For reprocessing the disaster relief operation a three phases approach will be applied. Following the example set by Kovács and Spens (2007), the operation will be divided into the phase before the catastrophe took place (the preparation phase), the phase instantly after the disaster (the immediate response phase) and the phase with a certain distance of time to the disaster (the reconstruction phase).

5.1.   Preparation for the Indian Ocean Tsunami in 2004

In regard of preparation, logistics functions are limited. In contrast, local communities and authorities play a major role in this phase since the local population has to respond immediately after a disaster occurs.

Therefore, to be able to evaluate the phase of preparation, it is important to question if governments and authorities of affected countries educated the locals adequately before the first waves of the tsunami reached the coasts.

In Sri Lanka, for example, there was little knowledge about the danger of tsunamis. In addition, the mainly poor, fishing based communities lived within a few kilometers of the beach. The combination of not-existing knowledge about the nature of tsunamis and the geographical residential area led to high casualty rates in the affected communities. (Perry, 2007)

While Sri Lanka was not prepared at all for the scenario of a tsunami, the government in Malaysia had installed tsunami sirens in areas more prone to be affected by such a disaster. Nevertheless, although an alert signal warned people staying in risk areas, the catastrophe hit the population surprisingly. The reason hereof is similar as it is in the case of Sri Lanka: People were not aware of the tsunami risk. (Aini, Fakhru´l-Razi, Ahmad-Rozi, & Fuad, 2011)

The carelessness of governments regarding to the education of the local population caused a high mortality rate. Experts criticized that no master plan led by the governments and no management approach involving the vulnerable communities existed. An involvement of local communities in the planning and decision making process to use the local expertise was demanded in the aftermath. (Perry, 2007)

In general, preparedness support was insufficient. Due to a lack of risk prevention, also the housing situation of communities was inadequate. To be prepared for tsunamis in the future it is necessary to include construction experts in the early preparation phase to ensure strategically planned, tsunami proofed housing on higher grounds. (Perry, 2007)

Basically, governments failed to warn the population in order to minimize the impacts of the tsunami. One reason for this might be that only two of the affected countries, Thailand and Indonesia, have already been equipped with a tsunami warning system developed for the Pacific Ocean. Installing a similar warning system for the Indian Ocean was discussed by governments before the tsunami in 2004; but this intention was never executed. (Symonds, 2005)

Simply put, the danger of tsunamis was underestimated for a long time by the governments. Based on the underrating of such an event, no investments in early-warning technologies were made. (Symonds, 2005)

But not only governments, also humanitarian aid agencies acknowledged some faults in terms of preparation. For instance, a misjudgment of the situation and an inadequate planning within many organizations brought along problems in the execution of the response. There was only little value placed on the strategic planning including a corporate strategy. Such a strategy could have clarified questions of transport and warehousing, which again would have facilitated the disaster response operation. (Beresford & Pettit, 2009)

Summarizing the findings concerning the phase of preparation one can state that there was a general lack of community knowledge based on poor educational efforts undertaken by the governments. Furthermore, governments failed to install adequate early-warning systems. As a result, the population could not be warned and those affected were hit surprisingly.

5.2.   Phase of Immediate Response

The phase of immediate response is very challenging for humanitarian aid agencies. Supply chains need to be designed and deployed at once even though the on-site situation is unknown. (Kovács & Spens, 2007) Once humanitarian organizations arrive in the crisis region, many influencing factors hamper a frictionless disaster operation.

In the case of the Indian Ocean tsunami, many problems occurred whereby a lack of cooperation and coordination among the parties involved needs to be emphasized. Therefore, the phase of immediate response will be further sectioned into the items: actors, cooperation/coordination and other issues.

5.2.1. Actors in the Phase of Immediate Response

As already mentioned, the Indian Ocean tsunami led to the largest response in the history of humanitarian aid. (Neri, Scuteri, & Miniati, 2008) This fact, in reverse, signifies that a great number of actors were involved. The necessary high participation of actors brought along avoidable and unavoidable problems.

For instance, in Indonesia approximately 400 international non government organizations were working to provide basic assistance. The tasks to fulfill for these organizations in the first days were broad based and ranged from providing transport access and basic survival requirements (such as clean water or cooking utensils and food) to medical attention and body identification. (Perry, 2007)

An insufficiency appeared in the assessment of the situation: International organizations relied on their own expertise without including local people in their assessment-teams. This circumstance led to misjudgments based on cultural differences. For example, in order to calculate the right volume of relief supplies for a community, it would have been more beneficial to investigate the number of survivors. Aid agencies, however, asked for the number of people living in a community. Natives assumed that the number of people living in a community before the tsunami occurred was asked. As a result, miscalculations were inevitable. (Perry, 2007)

Further, only 58 per cent of the organizations included logisticians in their planning and evaluation-teams, what again led to problems in the supply chain at a later date due to an improper information transfer concerning choke points. (Beresford & Pettit, 2009)

Additional evidence for a defective assessment of the situation was shown in a survey: While 72 per cent of the responding organizations had an assessment process to plan for relief in the tsunami region, 62 per cent of them stated that their plans failed to meet needs. (Whiting & Ayala-Öström, 2009)

Moreover, in the phase of immediate response, the majority of participants with logistics responsibilities did not have training in logistics before since many aid agencies tend to value field experience more than formal training in logistics. Surprised by the dimension of the tsunami, 88 per cent of the humanitarian aid agencies involved in the disaster relief operation had to relocate their most experienced logisticians from other operations. (Beresford & Pettit, 2009)

5.2.2. Cooperation and Coordination in the Phase of Immediate Response

Cooperation and coordination among humanitarian agencies was in need of improvement. A lack of cooperation based on self interest hindered a better coordination. Perry (2007) stated that "it was, however, apparent that some of the agencies guarded information to ensure their niche."

During the phase of immediate response, cooperation was only limited noticeable. On the other side, competitiveness disadvantaged aid agencies in general and led to an increase in transport costs. This increase of transport costs is attributable to the competition for the same transport capacity. Local transport sources, therefore, reacted to market forces and increased prices as demand outstripped supply. (Beresford & Pettit, 2009)

Since information was not shared in a proper extent, many non government organizations were working independently at the beginning. Information gathering was not only difficult because of lacking cooperation, also the remoteness of many affected coastal areas due to destruction of telecommunications systems, roads and bridges, had negative impacts. (Perry, 2007)

The United Nations Office for Coordination of Humanitarian Affairs took a leading role in the overall coordination and provided necessary information for organizations in affected areas by establishing Humanitarian Information Centers. The available information included maps and contact details of organizations. (Perry, 2007) Furthermore, coordination meetings were held regularly. For instance, in Banda Aceh, Indonesia, 72 meetings took place per week; however, this high number of meetings combined with the high level of attendance was criticized by several experts. (Tatham & Pettit, 2010)

Additionally, even though common information technology systems existed, aid agencies preferred to rely on traditional tools of communication: 50 per cent of organizations were using e-mail systems instead of common platforms. (Beresford & Pettit, 2009)

5.2.3. Other Issues in the Phase of Immediate Response

Another software based problem was the low usage of track and trace systems. While it is known that systems to track and trace relief commodities have the potential to improve the overall effectiveness of delivering aid (Beresford & Pettit, 2009), only 26 per cent of the organizations applied it for the Indian Ocean tsunami disaster relief operation. (Whiting & Ayala-Öström, 2009)

Further, the proliferation of non government organizations and volunteer groups in the affected regions contributed to the early confusion and oversupply of goods. The high quantities of donations led to logistical challenges. On one side, warehouse capacities were exhausted, on the other side a lack of suitable moving and transport equipment existed. A chaos emerged, what is also referable to the shortage of logistics expertise. (Perry, 2007)

5.3. Phase of Reconstruction

Once the phase of immediate response is finished, the phase of reconstruction starts. The duration of this phase usually takes at least as long as the prior livelihood situation of the affected population is restored. (Neri, Scuteri, & Miniati, 2008) Therefore, a sustainable redevelopment of the physical- and housing infrastructure is necessary.

Humanitarian organizations had to face infrastructural challenges that hampered reconstruction after the Indian Ocean tsunami. The poor infrastructure is attributable to two factors: First, the tsunami left behind devastation and chaos. Second, many regions affected by the tsunami already had a deficient infrastructure before the disaster occurred. (Chang, Wilkinson, Potangaroa, & Seville, 2012)

In general, non government organizations focused more on housing reconstruction and overlooked to invest in the development of the transport infrastructure. (Chang, Wilkinson, Potangaroa, & Seville, 2012) Thus, the transport of material in the aftermath of the tsunami was very time consuming due to infrastructural problems including ruined harbors, bridges and roads. (Braune & Goddar, 2009)

Within a few days after the tsunami, humanitarian agencies began to construct establishments for temporary housing. The focus thereby was on emergency handling and did not allow evaluation approaches. This circumstance is also attributable to the pressure caused by donors to deliver visible results as quickly as possible. The fact, that beneficiaries (affected locals) frequently were neither involved in the site selection nor in planning and decision making processes led to further frustration within the population. (Wiek, Ries, Thabrew, Brundiers, & Wickramasinghe, 2010)

In some cases, people needed to live in agency-provided tents for more than 12 months because of the high time exposure of reconstruction which was based, among others, on a lack of physical infrastructure. As a result, a long-term lack of trust and cooperation between the local population and aid agencies appeared. (Perry, 2007)

Another point of criticism was a lack of follow-up-plans to ensure a stable reconstruction in the aftermath of the tsunami. (Perry, 2007) It was also mentioned that long-term consideration of livelihood recovery from the very start, instead of pure emergency handling, was missing. A previous revitalization of the economical- and social activities of the affected population could have reduced the waste of emergency aid afterwards. (Neri, Scuteri, & Miniati, 2008)

5.3.1. Resource Availability in the Phase of Reconstruction

Besides infrastructural and interpersonal issues, resource availability is a main challenge in recovery projects. In the case of the Indian Ocean Tsunami, many factors affected an adequate availability of resources negative.

Generally, factors that influenced resource availability in the phase of reconstruction can be classified into five categories: factors related to the construction market, factors related to transportation, factors related to the reconstruction project, factors related to project stakeholders and factors related to the project operational environment. (Chang, Wilkinson, Potangaroa, & Seville, 2012)

A factor related to the construction market, for example, was the competition for resources. The influence of availability based on competition after the Indian Ocean tsunami was attributable to the high number of stakeholders involved including aid agencies, construction companies and affected communities. These stakeholders were in a competition for limited resources what resulted in a fluctuation of resource prices. Moreover, after a major disaster, existing market and procurement systems tend to be impaired and the existing local production system is mostly not able to cope with the recovery requirements. (Chang, Wilkinson, Potangaroa, & Seville, 2012)

A factor that influenced the availability of transport resources was the lack of transport capacity. In the case of the Indian Ocean tsunami, the high costs of transport due to limited port and shipping capacity combined with lengthy resource procurement times were major obstacles. (Chang, Wilkinson, Potangaroa, & Seville, 2012)

An example for factors related to the reconstruction project is that also the type of the project influences the availability of resources. The Indian Ocean tsunami had been a large scale natural disaster and the magnitude of the destruction led to a sudden increase in the demand of construction services. Especially housing projects were very challenging due to time pressure. Many aid agencies needed to acquire most commonly used materials simultaneously. (Chang, Wilkinson, Potangaroa, & Seville, 2012)

A factor related to project stakeholders emerged due to a lack of coordination among the procurement personnel of different agencies and a lack of communication between them and local authorities. Experts therefore demanded support from the government by regulating construction markets or providing training for practitioners. (Chang, Wilkinson, Potangaroa, & Seville, 2012)

The influence of the Indonesian government by implementing the "Green Aceh" timber administration rules is attributable to the factors related to the project operational environment. Because of this new regulation, timber needed to be imported from donor countries such as Australia, Canada and New Zealand. This included lead times of three to four months and therefore influenced long-term reconstruction work in Indonesia. (Chang, Wilkinson, Potangaroa, & Seville, 2012)

In a survey, executed between May and March 2008, 20 experts (including project managers of non government organizations, donor representatives and governmental officials) voted project stakeholder related factors followed by operational environment factors and construction market related factors as the most influencing factors for resource availability in Indonesia 2004. (Chang, Wilkinson, Potangaroa, & Seville, 2012)

An approach to minimize such influences is to establish collaborative procurement strategies. It is demanded that such strategies should be incorporated into the organizational cultures of humanitarian agencies to reduce the likelihood of competition for resources. (Chang, Wilkinson, Potangaroa, & Seville, 2012)

5.4. Improvements after the Indian Ocean Tsunami

The Indian Ocean tsunami can be seen as turning point in humanitarian logistics. Since many insufficiencies in every single phase of the disaster occurred, proposals for improvements were made and partly implemented.

In the aftermath of the tsunami, the Malaysian government invested in technology to be better prepared in the case of a similar future event. Thereby, a very important step was the installation of a tsunami early warning system. It ensures a timely and effective early warning to the population in the case of a tsunami generated over the Indian Ocean, South China Sea, Sulu Sea or Pacific Ocean. The system includes 15 seismic stations, 5 deep see buoys, 16 tidal gauges and 4 off shore cameras. (Aini, Fakhru´l-Razi, Ahmad-Rozi, & Fuad, 2011)

In addition, the Malaysian government marked evacuation routes to indicate the direction to the inland or to higher grounds. (Aini, Fakhru´l-Razi, Ahmad-Rozi, & Fuad, 2011)

The Thai government organized a simulated tsunami warning drill in December 2005 to prepare the local population for future tsunami scenarios. Many thousand participants along the Andaman coast contributed to the overall success of the simulation. In Indonesia the government installed sirens on phone towers to warn people staying in areas prone to be affected by a tsunami timely to ensure an adequate evacuation. (Perry, 2007)

Furthermore, organizations such as World Vision and the International Federation of the Red Cross started to realize the importance of prepositioning by maintaining fully stocked warehouses in risk areas and by negotiating pre-planned stock arrangements with suppliers and transport companies in selected countries. (Beresford & Pettit, 2009)

In terms of coordination an erroneous approach was obvious. Hence, efforts to reach necessary improvements were conducted. The Fritz Institute had an important role for reaching improvement in humanitarian logistics coordination by developing the "Humanitarian Logistics Software". (Whiting & Ayala-Öström, 2009)

This software was applied in the disaster relief operation after the Jakarta earthquake in 2006 and the results were promising. By comparing the data of the disaster relief operations in 2004 and 2006, supply chain set-up times have decreased from an average of 18 days to an average of 3 days. Furthermore, the software-support reduced the costs to deliver aid per family from approximately 800 US-Dollars to 142 US-Dollars (Whiting & Ayala-Öström, 2009) . In 2007, the Fritz Institute released a follow-up model of the "Humanitarian Logistics Software" named Helios. This model should contribute to further successes in terms of coordination in disaster relief operations. (Fritz Institute, 2007)

Further, the number of logistics conferences with the focus on humanitarian logistics has increased significantly since the Indian Ocean tsunami n 2004. As a result, international research groups and institution-specific research-teams were established. (Kovács & Spens, 2011)

Besides software-based progresses, affected countries developed emergency plans after the Indian Ocean tsunami. The aim of these plans is to ensure a systematic demand control. Moreover, these plans will facilitate the coordination between aid agencies and communities. (Aini, Fakhru´l-Razi, Ahmad-Rozi, & Fuad, 2011)

6. Conclusion

The tsunami in 2004 was the biggest natural catastrophe in the 21st century. The magnitude of the destruction led to the largest disaster relief operation in the history of humanitarian aid. The size of the impact seemed to surprise humanitarian organizations and therefore a lack of efficiency was unavoidable.

Perry (2007) outlined that insufficiencies were evident in the "overall preparedness for the tsunami, knowledge about local capabilities, requirements and vulnerabilities, coordination of needs assessments, levels of information sharing, collaboration amongst participating parties and the availability of logistical expertise".

The nonexistent evacuation directly before the first tsunami waves reached the coasts is attributable to the general naivety of the national governments. There were no early warning systems and the affected population was not aware of the dangers of a tsunami due to a lack of education. Shortly after the tsunami, governments decided to install an early warning system for the Indian Ocean. (Aini, Fakhru´l-Razi, Ahmad-Rozi, & Fuad, 2011)

The lack of cooperation and coordination needs to be emphasized due to the fact that it occurred in the phase of immediate response and in the phase of reconstruction. On one side, the reason for the bad coordination was partially based on self interest combined with a general unwillingness to share information. On the other side, also technology-based issues and the chaotic circumstances made coordination difficult. Positive developments in the information technology raise the hope for improvement in future disaster relief operations.

In conclusion it can be stated that the overall performance of humanitarian aid agencies was not as efficient as it should have been.

7. Bibliography

Abidi, H., de Leeuw, S., & Klumpp, M. (2014). Humanitarian supply chain performance management: a systematic literatur review. *Supply Chain Management: An International Journal, 19*(5/6), 592-608.

Aini, S., Fakhru´l-Razi, A., Ahmad-Rozi, M., & Fuad, A. (2011). Community preparedness for tsunami disaster: a case study. *Disaster Prevention and Management: An International Journal, 20*(3), 266-280.

b. (2007). *Fritz Institute releases Helios -- Groundbraking software to manage humanitarian organizations´relief chain*. Retrieved December 19, 2014, from http://www.fritzinstitute.org/prsrmPR-FI_ReleasesHELIOS.htm

Baumgartner, H., & Blome, H. (2014). *Bessere Hilfseinsätze*. Retrieved December 04, 2014, from E+Z Entwicklung und Zusammenarbeit Web site: http://www.dandc.eu/de/article/helmut-baumgarten-und-hendrik-blome-wie-die-logistik-bei-hilfseinsaetzen-krisenregionen

Beresford, A., & Pettit, S. (2009). Critical success factors in the context of humanitarian aid supply chains. *International Journal of Physical Distribution and Logistics Management, 39*(6), 450-468.

Braune, S., & Goddar, J. (2009). *Tsunami Report; Eine Fünf-Jahres-Bilanz*. Retrieved December 18, 2014, from Deutsches Rotes Kreuz Web site: http://www.drk.de/fileadmin/Presse/Downloads/Text/4-11-2009%20Tsunami-Report%20final.pdf

Chandes, J., & Paché, G. (2010). Investigating humanitarian logistics issues: from operations management to strategic action. *Journal of Manufacturing Technology Management, 21*(3), 320-340.

Chang, Y., Wilkinson, S., Potangaroa, R., & Seville, E. (2012). Managing resources in disaster recovery projects. *Engineering, Construction and Architectural Management, 19*(5), 557-580.

Fagotto, M. (2014). *10 years later: Indonesian survivors of the 2004 Indian Ocean tsunami recall their stories*. Retrieved December 15, 2014, from The National Web site: http://www.thenational.ae/arts-lifestyle/the-review/10-years-later-indonesian-survivors-of-the-2004-indian-ocean-tsunami-recall-their-stories

Fawcett, A., & Fawcett, S. (2013). Benchmarking the state of humanitarian aid and disaster relief: A systems design perspective and research agenda. *Benchmarking: An International Journal, 20*(5), 661-692.

Fritz Institute. (2007). *Fritz Institute releases Helios -- Groundbreaking software to manage humanitarian organizations' relief chain.* Retrieved December 19, 2014, from Fritz Institute web site: http://www.fritzinstitute.org/prsrmPR-FI_ReleasesHELIOS.htm

Kovács, G., & Spens, K. (2007). Humanitarian logistics in disaster relief operations. *International Journal of Physical Distribution and Logistics Management, 37*(2), 99-114.

Kovacs, G., & Spens, K. (2009). Identifying challenges in humanitarian logistics. *International Journal of Physical Distribution & Logistics Management*(39 (6)), 506-528.

Kovács, G., & Spens, K. (2011). Trends and developments in humanitarian logistics - a gap analyis. *International Journal of Physical Distribution and Logistics Management, 41*(1), 32-45.

Langley, J., & Rutner, S. (2000). Logistics Value: Diefinition, Process and Measurement. *The International Journal of Logistics Management, 11*(2), 73-82.

Maon, F., Lindgreen, A., & Vanhamme, J. (2009). Developing supply chains in disaster relief operations through cross-sector socially oriented collaborations: A theoretical model. *Supply Chain Management: An International Journal, 14*(2), 149-164.

Neri, P., Scuteri, S., & Miniati, S. (2008). From emergency relief to livelihood recovery: Lessons learned from post-tsunami experiences in Indonesia and India. *Disaster Prevention and Management: An International Journal, 17*(3), 410-430.

Perry, M. (2007). Natural disaster management planning: A study of logistics managers responding to the tsunami. *International Journal of Physical Distribution and Logistics Management, 37*(5), 409-433.

Phillips, B., Nael, D., Wikle, T., Subanthore, A., & Hyrapiet, S. (2008). Mass fatality management after the Indian Ocean tsunami. *Disaster Prevention and Management: An International Journal, 17*(5), 681-697.

Scholten, K., Sharkey, P., & Fynes, S. (2010). (Le)agility in humanitarian aid (NGO) supply chains. *International Journal of Physical Distribution and Logistics Management, 40*(8/9), 623-635.

Sheppard, A., Tatham, P., Fisher, R., & Gapp, R. (2013). Humanitarian logistics: enhancing the engagement of local populations. *Journal of Humanitarian Logistics and Supply Chain Management, 3*(1), 22-36.

Symonds, P. (2005). *The Asian tsunami: why there were no warnings.* Retrieved December 16, 2014, from World Socialist Website.

Tatham, P., & Pettit, S. (2010). Transforming humanitarian logistics: the journey to supply network management. *International Journal of Physical Distribution and Logistics Management, 40*(8/9), 609-622.

Thomas, A., & Mizushima, M. (2005). Logistics Training: necessity or luxury? *Forced Migration Review*(22), 60.

Whiting, M., & Ayala-Öström, B. (2009). Advocacy to promote logistics in humanitarian aid. *Management Research News, 32*(11), 1081-1089.

Wiek, A., Ries, R., Thabrew, L., Brundiers, K., & Wickramasinghe, A. (2010). Challenges of sustainable recovery processes in tsunami affected communities. *Disaster Prevention and Management: An International Journal, 19*(4), 423-437.